FASHION MATH

MATH 24/7

Banking Math

Business Math

Computer Math

Culinary Math

Fashion Math

Game Math

Shopping Math

Sports Math

Time Math

Travel Math

MATH 24/7

FASHION MATH

RAE SIMONS

Mason Crest

Mason Crest
450 Parkway Drive, Suite D
Broomall, PA 19008
www.masoncrest.com

Printed in the United States of America.

First printing
9 8 7 6 5 4 3 2 1

Series ISBN: 978-1-4222-2901-9
ISBN: 978-1-4222-2906-4
ebook ISBN: 978-1-4222-8917-4

The Library of Congress has cataloged the
        hardcopy format(s) as follows:

                Library of Congress Cataloging-in-Publication Data

Simons, Rae, 1957-
  Fashion math / Rae Simons.
      pages cm. – (Math 24/7)
  Includes index.
    ISBN 978-1-4222-2906-4 (hardcover) – ISBN 978-1-4222-2901-9 (series) –
ISBN 978-1-4222-8917-4 (ebook)
  1. Fashion–Mathematics–Juvenile literature. I. Title.
  TT497.S49 2014
  746.9'20151–dc23
                        2013015665

Produced by Vestal Creative Services.
www.vestalcreative.com

Contents

INTRODUCTION

How would you define math? It's not as easy as you might think. We know math has to do with numbers. We often think of it as a part, if not the basis, for the sciences, especially natural science, engineering, and medicine. When we think of math, most of us imagine equations and blackboards, formulas and textbooks.

But math is actually far bigger than that. Think about examples like Polykleitos, the fifth-century Greek sculptor, who used math to sculpt the "perfect" male nude. Or remember Leonardo da Vinci? He used geometry—what he called "golden rectangles," rectangles whose dimensions were visually pleasing—to create his famous *Mona Lisa*.

Math and art? Yes, exactly! Mathematics is essential to disciplines as diverse as medicine and the fine arts. Counting, calculation, measurement, and the study of shapes and the motions of physical objects: all these are woven into music and games, science and architecture. In fact, math developed out of everyday necessity, as a way to talk about the world around us. Math gives us a way to perceive the real world—and then allows us to manipulate the world in practical ways.

For example, as soon as two people come together to build something, they need a language to talk about the materials they'll be working with and the object that they would like to build. Imagine trying to build something—anything—without a ruler, without any way of telling someone else a measurement, or even without being able to communicate what the thing will look like when it's done!

The truth is: We use math every day, even when we don't realize that we are. We use it when we go shopping, when we play sports, when we look at the clock, when we travel, when we run a business, and even when we cook. Whether we realize it or not, we use it in countless other ordinary activities as well. Math is pretty much a 24/7 activity!

And yet lots of us think we hate math. We imagine math as the practice of dusty, old college professors writing out calculations endlessly. We have this idea in our heads that math has nothing to do with real life, and we tell ourselves that it's something we don't need to worry about outside of math class, out there in the real world.

But here's the reality: Math helps us do better in many areas of life. Adults who don't understand basic math applications run into lots of problems. The Federal Reserve, for example, found that people who went bankrupt had an average of one and a half times more debt than their income—in other words, if they were making $24,000 per year, they had an average debt of $36,000. There's a basic subtraction problem there that should have told them they were in trouble long before they had to file for bankruptcy!

As an adult, your career—whatever it is—will depend in part on your ability to calculate mathematically. Without math skills, you won't be able to become a scientist or a nurse, an engineer or a computer specialist. You won't be able to get a business degree—or work as a waitress, a construction worker, or at a checkout counter.

Every kind of sport requires math too. From scoring to strategy, you need to understand math—so whether you want to watch a football game on television or become a first-class athlete yourself, math skills will improve your experience.

And then there's the world of computers. All businesses today—from farmers to factories, from restaurants to hair salons—have at least one computer. Gigabytes, data, spreadsheets, and programming all require math comprehension. Sure, there are a lot of automated math functions you can use on your computer, but you need to be able to understand how to use them, and you need to be able to understand the results.

This kind of math is a skill we realize we need only when we are in a situation where we are required to do a quick calculation. Then we sometimes end up scratching our heads, not quite sure how to apply the math we learned in school to the real-life scenario. The books in this series will give you practice applying math to real-life situations, so that you can be ahead of the game. They'll get you started—but to learn more, you'll have to pay attention in math class and do your homework. There's no way around that.

But for the rest of your life—pretty much 24/7—you'll be glad you did!

1
SIZE MATH

Maricela and a bunch of her friends are on a shopping trip. They all decide to go to the mall together, for a fun day. Maricela needs a few clothes too—she needs a new pair of jeans. Her friend Jason is looking for some t-shirts. And her friend Jacqui has to buy a new dress for a school dance.

Maricela really likes going shopping, because she gets to hang out with her friends. However, she gets frustrated sometimes when she can't find anything that fits. She spends hours in one store trying on dozens of clothes, since she never knows what will fit.

One way she could think about clothes sizes is in averages. If she knows her average clothing size, she can more easily find clothes that might fit her. On the next pages, you can explore averages and clothing size.

Maricela thinks of the last few times she's bought jeans. She has jeans of different sizes at home. She has one pair that is a junior's size 9, two that are size 11, one that is size 13, and one that is size 15.

To find the average size of her jeans, add up all the sizes and divide by the number of jeans.

1. What is Maricela's average jean size?

The average you get when you do the math is a decimal, not a whole number. Clothing sizes only come in whole numbers. In Maricela's case, she wears junior's sizes, which only come in odd numbers. In this case, her average size will be the odd number closest to her calculated average.

2. What is the closest junior's size to Maricela's calculated average?

Now Maricela knows which size to start trying on first.

You can also find the average sizes for the clothes her friends are trying to buy.

Jason has 3 t-shirts at home in small, 5 in medium, 1 in large, and 1 in extra large. You can't do averages using words, but you can assign each size a number.

$$Small = 1$$
$$Medium = 2$$
$$Large = 3$$
$$Extra\ large = 4$$

Now do the average.

3. What is Jason's average t-shirt size? You may have to round to the nearest whole number.

Now find the average dress size Jacqui should be looking for. She has 1 dress at home that is small, 1 that is medium, and 3 that are large.

4. What is Jacqui's average dress size?

2
MORE SIZE MATH: CONVERSIONS

In the second store Maricela and her friends go into, she finds three pairs of jeans she wants to try on. The trouble is, she doesn't recognize the sizes. She normally wears a size 11 in juniors, or sometimes a size 13. These jeans don't come in junior's sizes. Instead, two of the pairs she wants to try on are in women's sizes, and one is in European sizing.

Maricela is worried she'll have to try on every pair of jeans in the store to find one that fits. However, a store clerk comes over and offers to help. The store clerk tells her how to convert junior's sizes to women's and European sizes. Women's sizes are slightly smaller, and European sizes are based on waist measurement. Check out the next page to follow what Maricela learned.

First, the store clerk shows Maricela how to convert junior's sizes to women's sizes. She explains that junior's jeans are usually slimmer. She tells Maricela that women's sizes are usually about 3 numbers smaller than junior's sizes.

So, if Maricela usually wears an 11, she may wear an 8 in women's sizes. Of course, that won't always be true because the size of jeans is a little different from company to company. But it gives Maricela a place to start.

1. What size in women's jeans should Jacqui wear, if she normally wears a size 17 in juniors?

Now the store clerk explains how European sizing works. For jeans, the size number is how big around the waist is. Someone with a 26-inch waist would wear a size 26.

The store clerk takes out a tape measure and measures Maricela's waist, which is 38.5 inches. Then she shows her a chart that looks like this:

U.S. Junior's size	European size
1	28
3	30
5	32
7	34
9	36
11	38
13	40
15	42

2. What European size in jeans should Maricela try on first?

Jason decides he wants to try on some jeans too. Men's sizes are different from women's and juniors, though, so he can't follow the same rules as Maricela.

He finds a pair of jeans in a European size. The sales clerk tells him he can subtract 16 from the size on the tag to find the U.S. men's size.

3. Jason normally wears a size 36 in men's. The tag says the jeans he's holding are a size 42. Should he try them on? Why or why not?

Jason can add 16 to his usual size to figure out what European size he should look for.

4. What size should he look for?

4
SPENDING MONEY

Maricela and her friends have found a few things to buy, and they have spent some of their money. Maricela found a pair of jeans. Jacqui bought a dress and some shoes to go with it. Jason hasn't had as much luck and still needs a few new t-shirts.

The three friends aren't ready to leave the mall yet. They want to keep shopping for a little while. They have more to spend, although they want to save a little at the end to get ice cream in the food court.

Figure out how much they can spend on the next page, and if they will have enough left over for ice cream.

Maricela started out with $56 she had saved up from her allowance. She spent $24.93 on a pair of jeans, and also bought two pairs of earrings for $6.70 each. She still wants to buy a scarf, and have money left over for ice cream, which she thinks will be about $6.

Add up all the money she has spent, and subtract it from the total money she has to spend.

1. How much can Maricela spend on the scarf if she wants money left over for ice cream?

Jason can't quite remember how much money he has spent so far. He takes a look at his receipts and adds them up.

He finds receipts for:

sunglasses: $14.56
jeans: $27.23

He wants to spend less than $60, but he's not sure how much he has left to spend on t-shirts.

How many t-shirts can he buy with the money he has left, if they cost $7.50 each?

First, you need to see how much money he has left:

2. $60 − ($14.56 + $27.23) =

Next, divide your answer by $7.50, the cost of a t-shirt. Round down to the nearest whole number.

3. How many t-shirts can he buy with the money he has left?

4. How many t-shirts can he buy if he wants to save at least $5 for ice cream? Remember, he can only buy t-shirts in whole numbers (since he can't buy half a t-shirt!). How much will he have left in total?

5
SALES MATH

Maricela is starting to worry she's spending too much money. Maybe she shouldn't spend everything she has saved up for the shopping trip. She might need it later for something else.

She still wants to buy a scarf, though. She thinks her best bet is to find a good sale. Everywhere she's gone in the mall, she has seen signs for sales of 10%, 25%, and even 50% off. She asks her friends to help her on her sale hunt.

The next store they go into, they see sale signs right away. The signs tell them that clothes with different colored tags have different sales prices:

Blue: 5% off
Orange: 15% off
Red: 25% off
Green: 50% off
Yellow: 75% off

What is the best deal? Find out on the next page.

You found in the last section that Maricela has $12.67 to spend on a scarf. She wants to spend less than that if possible. Maricela first finds a scarf that originally cost $21.99. It has a red tag. Can she afford it?

You can think about percents in a few ways. The red tag means the scarf is 25% off. Another way of think about 25% is one-fourth of something. The price of the scarf costs one-fourth less. Divide the price by 4 to find out the discount.

1. $21.99/4 =

You're not done yet. Now you know how many dollars less the scarf is. You still have to subtract the number you go from the full price of the scarf.

2. What is the final discounted price? Can Maricela buy it?

Maricela finds another scarf that was $55.60, but has a yellow tag. It used to be expensive, but now it's 75% off!

This time, use cross multiplication to figure out if she can buy it: 75% off is the same as saying 75 out of 100. Here's how you figure it out:

$$75/100 = X/\$55.60$$
$$100 \times X = \$55.60 \times 75$$
$$X = \$41.70$$

The scarf is 75% off, so you have to subtract $41.70 from the original price.

You could also convert the percent to a decimal. Just move the decimal place to the left two spaces.

$$75\% = 0.75$$

Then multiply the cost by the percent, and subtract that number from the original cost. Try it:

3. 0.75 x $55.60 =

4. How much money does this scarf cost? Can she afford it?

5. Finally, Maricela finds another scarf that cost $20.40, and is 50% off.

6. Can she buy this one? How much will she have left if she can buy it? Use whatever method you want to figure it out.

6
SHOPPING ONLINE

When Maricela gets home from shopping at the mall, she realizes she forgot to buy her dad a birthday present! He told her he needs a new tie, because all his other ones are wearing out. She really doesn't want to go back to the mall. Instead, she sits down at the computer to find her dad a tie online.

Once Maricela finds the perfect tie, she's ready to buy it. The tie Maricela picks costs $16.99 online. She thinks she's getting a good deal until she remembers she has to pay tax and shipping and handling. Tax is money the government charges and collects every time someone makes a purchase. Shipping and handling is the money she'll have to pay to get the tie sent to her in the mail.

She doesn't have a debit card or credit card of her own, so she asks her mom to pay online for her. Maricela also spent almost all her money at the mall, so she also has to borrow money from her mom for the present. Figure out how much Maricela has to borrow, and how she's going to pay for the present online on the following pages.

The tax on clothes in Maricela's state is 9.5%. This is a percent just like the sales percents you worked with before. However, this time it's a percent to add on to the cost of the tie, not a percent to subtract away.

1. How much does the tie cost with tax added on?

Now you have to add on the shipping and handling to get the full price of the tie bought online.

2. If the shipping and handling is $4.99, how much is the final price of the tie?

Maricela doesn't have that much money to give her mom yet.

3. Using your answer from section 5, how much money does Maricela need to get to pay her mom?

Maricela agrees to pay her mom back in installments. Every week, she will give her $5. That will give her enough time to save up money.

Use the chart below to figure out how many weeks it will take her to pay her mom back. Fill in the rest of the chart until you get to $0. You may not need to use all the rows.

Week	Original amount	Amount Left to Be Paid
1	$23.59	$18.59
2	$18.59	$13.59
3	$13.59	

4. How many weeks will it take Maricela to pay her mom back?

19

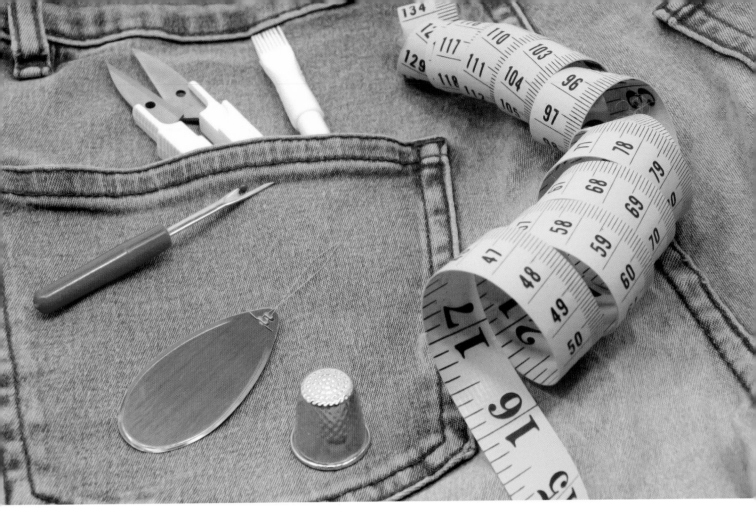

7
TAILORING

O nce she tries on her new jeans at home again, Maricela realizes they don't quite fit. They fit her waist fine, but they are too long. She tries turning them up at the bottom, but they end up looking silly.

She doesn't want to return them. Besides, she already ripped the tag off. Her mom suggests she take them to the tailor around the corner. The tailor, her mom explains, will take her measurements, and then fix the jeans so they are the right length. Shortening pants is called hemming, in the tailoring world.

Maricela and her mom go to the tailor's and bring the jeans along. Her mom also brings a jacket that has gotten too tight. She doesn't want to get rid of it, and she thinks the tailor can alter it enough so it fits again.

The tailor, Mrs. Shah, brings Maricela and her mom to the back room. First she measures how long Maricela's legs are. Then she measures her mom's waist, where the jacket has gotten too tight. She tells them the jeans and the jacket will be ready the next day, and that they are easy fixes!

For the jeans, Mrs. Shah measures from the very top of the inseam (the seam that runs up the middle of the jeans, on the inside of the legs) to the bottom of the inseam. The bottom is where Maricela's pants will end. Maricela's inseam measures 28½ inches.

After they leave, Mrs. Shah measures the inseam of the jeans Maricela left. The inseam is 30¾ inches.

1. What is the difference between Maricela's actual leg length and the jeans?

This is how much Mrs. Shah will hem up the jeans. She wants to fold back the fabric so that the bottoms of the jeans are now at the right length.

Mrs. Shah will fold up the bottom of the jeans twice, so the original hem is completely hidden.

How many inches should she fold up each time? You will have to divide a fraction. Turn the total number of inches into an improper fraction. Then divide that number by two (because she is folding twice), and turn your answer back into a proper fraction.

2. What do you get?

Mrs. Shah folds up the hem and sews all around. Maricela's jeans are done!

Next, Mrs. Shah has to make Maricela's mom's jacket bigger by letting out the seams, the places where the sweater is sewed together.

Maricela's mom's waist was 41 inches around. When the jacket is buttoned, it is 41¼ inches around. The tailor has to make the jacket ¾ of an inch bigger, so that it won't feel so snug.

It's not actually as hard as it sounds. The tailor just has to rip out a seam and sew it back again, making sure she sews closer to the edge to give Maricela's mom more room. She will resew each side.

3. If she wants to let out the seams at total of ¾ of an inch, and she wants to let out that amount evenly on each of two sides, how much more room should each side have?

8
RESELLING OLD CLOTHES

While the tailor is fixing up the jeans, Maricela goes through her closet. She has a lot of clothes! She has barely even worn any of them. Those shirts in the back look great, she thinks—why hasn't she ever worn them? She takes them out and tries them on. They don't fit. She bought them a few years ago, and now they're too small for her.

Maricela starts a pile of clothes she wants to get rid of because they're too small, or she doesn't wear them anymore. She tosses in her old pair of jeans she just replaced, along with the shirts, and some other clothes.

She definitely doesn't want to throw all these clothes away, because someone can still wear them. Then she remembers her cousin telling her about reselling his old clothes to a consignment store. He brought his old clothes in, and the store took the ones that were in good enough shape. Then every time the store sold something he had brought in, it would give him a little money.

Maricela also remembers the used clothing store where she shops sometimes. You can bring old clothes there, and they pay you for the items that are in the best shape. The secondhand store is picky, but Maricela might have a couple things she could sell. Figure out how much she makes reselling her clothes on the next page.

Maricela first visits the second-hand store. She looks at the prices she could get for her clothes:

t-shirts: $3
button-up shirts: $4
sweaters: $5
pants: $5
skirts: $4
dresses: $6
jewelry: $3
jackets: $10

Maricela has brought in 3 pairs of pants, 4 t-shirts, 1 button-up shirt, 2 dresses, and 1 necklace.

1. What is the most she can make from the secondhand store?

The cashier looks over her things and accepts 1 pair of pants, 3 t-shirts, 1 dress, and the necklace.

2. How much did she make?

Next, Maricela heads over to the consignment store. It seems like it accepts clothes that aren't necessarily in perfect condition, so she hopes it will take everything she has left.

The consignment store gives people 20% of the price that the clothing sells for.

It ends up taking everything Maricela has. The woman there tells Maricela the prices she will use to sell each piece:

2 pairs of pants: $5.99 each
1 t-shirt: $2.99
1 button-up shirt: $4.50
1 dress: $8.75

3. How much will Maricela make if all these clothes are sold?

9

SEWING: CIRCUMFERENCE AND DIAMETER

Ever since she went to the tailor, Maricela has been thinking how cool it would be to sew her own clothes. She loves art, and has tried knitting and crocheting. She could save money and do something creative if she sewed her own clothes.

Maricela does some research and decides she wants to sew a simple circle skirt. She will need just one kind of fabric, and she will only have to make a few cuts. The basic idea is that she will cut out a circle. Then she will cut out a hole in the middle, as big as her waist. Then she will sew a waist on it, and hem the bottom.

The directions say she has to decide how long a skirt she wants. She chooses to make a skirt that is 18 inches long. Now she has to do some math to figure out how much fabric she needs to maker her skirt. Her goal is to find out the diameter—how wide the circle is—so she can figure how much cloth to buy.

For a skirt that is 18 inches long, she has to measure out 18 inches from the edge of the big circle to the outside edge of the little circle she will cut out in the middle.

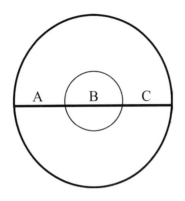

First she measures how wide her waist is. From the mall, she knows her waist is 38.5 inches around, which is the circumference of her waist. She can use that information to figure out how wide it is.

The formula for circumference is

$$C = \pi \times d$$

C is circumference, d is the diameter, and π is pi, or 3.14. You can rearrange the formula to give you diameter instead:

$$d = C/\pi$$

1. What is the diameter of Maricela's waist?

Now Maricela knows how big the hole in the middle should be (line B). Next she has to calculate how big the entire circle should be.

She wants the skirt to hang 18 inches down, so she has to make lines A and C at least 18 inches long. She also has to hem it, so she should add an extra 0.5 inch on either side.

Now she must add all the lengths together to find the total diameter of the circle, even with the hole in the middle.

2. What is the total diameter?

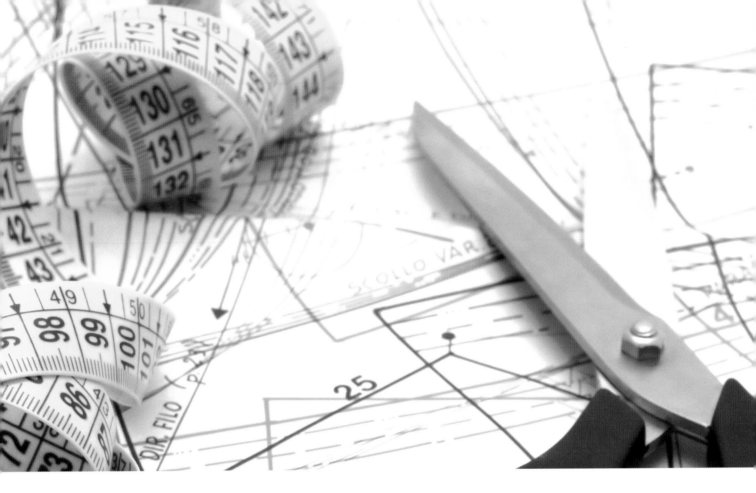

10
SEWING: RECTANGULAR DIMENSIONS

Maricela is very excited about her new hobby. Besides the skirt, she also wants to try designing and sewing a simple handbag. Her friend Jonathan at school made his own backpack. She doesn't think she's ready for that yet, but she thinks she could handle a small purse.

She looks at patterns online and sees that she could sew a bag made mostly out of rectangles sewn together. She wants to design her own bag to see if she really understands sewing. She takes out a piece of paper and starts drawing rectangles she will sew together into a bag, shown on the following page.

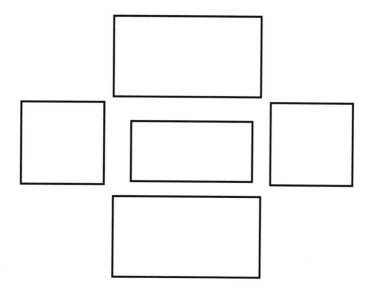

Maricela has her simple design, but she needs to figure out the dimensions. She has to know how big to cut the rectangles out of fabric so she can sew them together.

She starts with the center rectangle in her drawing, which will be the bottom of the bag. She just wants a small bag, so she makes the length (the longer end) 8 inches, and the width (the shorter end) 4 inches.

Then she realizes she has to add on a little bit for the seam, where it will get sewn to the other pieces. She adds ¼ inch all the way around, making the dimensions 8¼ by 4¼ inches.

The other pieces have to fit around the middle rectangle to make the sides. Maricela decides she wants the bag to be 5 inches tall, which will help her determine how big the other pieces are.

The smaller end pieces will have to be 5¼ inches long, to match how tall she wants the bag. They will also be 4¼ inches wide, to match the width of the middle rectangle.

1. How long should the larger end pieces be, and why?

2. How wide should the middle pieces be, and why?

   She will also need a long, skinny rectangle for the handle, which will be 24 inches long and 2½ inches wide.

11
CHOOSING FABRIC

Maricela still needs to do a little more planning before she can actually start sewing her skirt and bag. She needs to figure out how much fabric she needs to buy. If she buys too much, then she wastes her money by buying something she doesn't need. If she buys too little, she won't be able to make her projects.

Figuring out the amount of fabric she needs means thinking about dimensions and also area, or how much room a shape takes up. Dimensions will help her out with the circle, while area is useful with her rectangular bag project. How will she figure it out?

Maricela knows the diameter of the big circle she will cut out for her skirt. You just calculated it in section 9.

Now think about the fabric. It comes on a roll that is 45 inches wide by however many yards long you need.

1. Is 45 inches wide big enough for the diameter of the circle? If so, how much extra fabric will there be?

Will a piece of fabric that is 45 inches by 1 yard be long enough? One way to figure it out is to see if 1 yard is longer than the diameter of the circle. Convert 1 yard to feet and then inches with this information:

$$1 \text{ yard} = 3 \text{ feet}, 1 \text{ foot} = 12 \text{ inches}$$

2. Is 1 yard long enough? If not, how many more inches will Maricela need?

Yards also come in quarters and halves. One-quarter yard is:

$$.25 \text{ yards x } 3 \text{ feet x } 12 \text{ inches} = 9 \text{ inches.}$$

3. Will a yard and a quarter fit the diameter of the circle?

Now Maricela needs to buy fabric for her bag. She knows the area of a rectangle is:

$$A = \text{length x width}$$

She needs to add up all the areas of the rectangles she's going to cut out, and then get fabric with an area that is at least as large as that. Remember, ¼ inch is the same as saying .25 inches

4. What do all the areas of the rectangles add up to in square inches?

Now calculate the area in square inches of a piece of fabric that is 45 inches by ½ yard long:

5. 45 inches x (.5 yard x 3 feet x 12 inches) =

6. Is that enough fabric? If not, how much more does she need? If so, could she get ¼ yard and have enough?

12

FASHION BUSINESS: FIGURING OUT PRICES

Maricela discovers she really likes sewing clothes. Plus, she's pretty good at it. Her friends all really like her clothes, and soon they're asking if she can make them clothes too.

At first, Maricela really enjoys making clothes for her friends. She gets to practice, and she makes her friends happy. However, all the materials and supplies she has to buy really add up over time. She pays for everything herself, and she's going to be broke soon!

She's thinking about starting to sell her clothes to make some money. She might start selling at local craft fairs, or maybe set up a website and sell them online. Before she does that, she needs to figure out how much her clothes should be. She will have to add up all the costs of making them. To make a profit, she will need to price them higher than the cost of making them. Plus, she will need to figure out how much she thinks her time and skills are worth, and add that on to the price.

Maricela sets up a log to keep track of her sewing expenses. She creates one log for each sewing project.

Here's a log for her last project, a dress.

Item	Cost
Needles	$4.98
Thread, 5 spools	$7.45
Fabric	$26.23

1. What was her total cost for this project?

She takes another look at her costs. She didn't have to buy the needles or thread specifically for this project. She'll end up using both of those for many projects, not just this one. Her only cost specifically for the dress was the fabric.

2. How much do you think she needs at least to charge to make a profit on this dress?

Now she will calculate how much she thinks her time is worth, to get the whole price.

She spent 15 hours sewing the dress. Those 15 hours were spent sewing, not doing anything else. In fact, she could have been making money. Some of her friends have jobs at the mall, or at restaurants. They make about $9 an hour.

3. How much would Maricela have made in the time she sewed her dress if she were working at a store in the mall for $9 an hour?

Maricela adds how much money she could have been making to the cost of making the dress for a possible price. She takes a look to see if the price makes sense.

4. Do you think customers would pay that price for a dress? Is it too cheap or too expensive?

Maricela decides to make the dress cheaper, so that she can convince people to buy it. She is a new sewer after all. As her skills get better and better, she can charge higher prices.

She will charge a price that is 35% of the price she just calculated.

5. How much is the new price? Do you think it seems fair to customers and to Maricela?

13
SELLING ON COMMISSION

Maricela just heard about a new shop in town that sells people's artwork and crafts. They offer space for people to sell paintings, knit scarves, clothes, and more. The new store sells by commission. That is, they take some of the money from the sale, although most of it goes to the maker. Maricela never thought she would be able to sell her clothes in a store!

She goes and talks to the manager of the store, Tomás. Tomás tells her the shop takes a 15% commission from the sale of clothes. In other words, for every piece of clothing she sells, the store will get 15% of it. Tomás tells her that the store will set the price of her clothes. They know what customers will spend, and can make prices to reflect that.

Maricela is a little nervous—what if the store sets the price really low? She doesn't need to worry, though, because Tomás tells her he will set the price at $75 a dress, $50 a shirt, $50 a skirt, and $40 a bag. Those are higher prices than she was selling her clothes at before! She is a really good fashion designer and sewer.

Finish filling out this chart to see how much money Maricela will make when her clothes sell:

Item	Price	Store Commission	Rest
Dress	$75	$11.25	$63.75
Shirt			
Skirt			
Bag			

1. Will Maricela make more money from selling her dress at the store than she was making before? If so, how much more? If not, how much less?

2. If Maricela spends $16.50 on fabric for a bag, what will her profit be?

3. How many shirts would she have to sew to make at least $150 in profit?

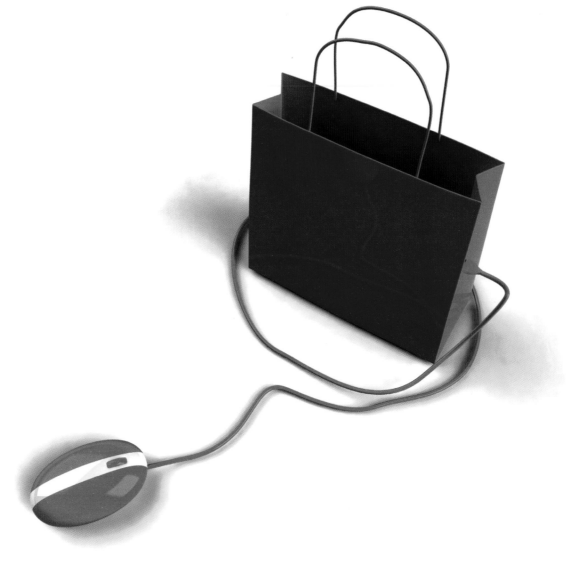

14
SELLING ONLINE

Selling clothes at the store is fun, but Maricela wants to reach more people. Only the customers who go in the store are seeing her clothes, but she thinks more people might be interested in buying them. When Maricela first started thinking about selling her clothes, she wanted to sell them online. Now is a good time to start!

First she considers setting up her own website, but she would have to work really hard to get people to come to her site in the first place. Another option is to sell her clothes on a virtual marketplace: a website someone else has set up for artists and crafters to sell what they make.

She signs up for a craft website and reads their rules. They will charge her $.20 for every thing she lists, and then take a 3.5% commission. She will have to come up with how much to charge in shipping and handling, to send the clothes to buyers. It seems like a lot of numbers! The next page will show how Maricela figures it all out.

First, Maricela wants to see how much she will make from online sales. She can set her own prices, so she decides to go with the prices the art shop set for her clothes.

How much money will she make, considering the costs she has to pay to the website? Take a look at a dress she will be selling for $75.

Costs:
$.20 for listing the dress online
3.5% x $75 = $2.63

1. How much will she make in total on the dress? How much of that will be profits if she spends $28.30 on the fabric?

Now calculate the shipping and handling using the following information:

- the dress weighs 15 ounces
- the box the dress will be packed in weighs 6 ounces
- the box costs $1.99
- the post office charges $.35 an ounce

How much should Maricela charge for shipping and handling for the dress?

total weight: 15 ounces + 6 ounces = 21 ounces
price based on weight: 21 ounces x $.35 = $7.35
price with box: $7.35 + $1.99 = 9.34

2. How much money will the customer have to pay including shipping and handling?

If someone in another country wants to buy the dress, the shipping and handling go up. The post office automatically charges $12, plus $.60 an ounce.

3. How much would an international customer pay in shipping and handling?

15
PUTTING IT ALL TOGETHER

Maricela has come a long way from her shopping trip at the mall. She has learned how clothes sizes work, how to keep track of the money she spends on clothes, how to design and sew clothes, and how to sell clothes to customers.

Someday, Maricela wants to go to school for fashion design and become a big name in fashion. She's well on her way by now, because she is learning so much math! See if you can remember what Maricela has learned along the way.

1. What size would a girl wear in U.S. junior sizes if she were a European size 32?

2. What size shoe would a boy wear if his feet (with socks) were 9¾ inches long?

3. While you are shopping for a sweatshirt, you find one that is on sale for 40% off. The original cost is $32.99. How much is it after the discount?

4. The sales tax on the sweatshirt is 9.5%. Can you afford it if you only have $25 to spend? Why or why not?

5. If a pair of pants is 29 inches, and the person who wants to wear them has an inseam of 26 inches, should the pants be hemmed?

   If so, by how much?

6. You give an old shirt to a consignment store. They price it at $6.50 and offer you 20%. How much will you get?

7. The area of the fabric you need to sew a shirt is 825 square inches. The craft store only has a half of a yard of the fabric you want to use. Will it be enough?

If not, how much more fabric do you need?

8. You spend $8.80 on fabric for a sewing project. You sell it for $20.

How much is your profit?

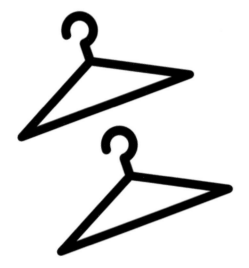

FIND OUT MORE IN BOOKS

Andrus, Aubre. *Math + Fashion = Fun*. Middleton, Wisc.: American Girl Publishing, 2012.

Bertoletti, John C. *How Fashion Designers Use Math*. New York: Chelsea Clubhouse, 2009.

Ferguson. *Fashion (Discovering Careers for Your Future)*. New York: Ferguson Publishing Company, 2004.

Minden, Cecilia. *Smart Shopping (Real World Math: Personal Finance)*. North Mankato, Minn.: Cherry Lake Publishing, 2007.

Sadler, Judy Ann. *Simply Sewing*. Tonawanda, N.Y.: Kids Can Press, 2004.

ANSWERS

1.

1. $(9 + 11 + 11 + 13 + 15)/5 = 11.8$
2. 11
3. His average is 2, which is medium.
4. medium

2.

1. Size 14
2. 38
3. No, because they are only a size 26 in U.S. men's size.
4. A 52 in European size.

3.

1. 78
2. $7\frac{6}{8} + \frac{3}{8} = 8\frac{1}{8}$
   $8\frac{1}{8} = 10\frac{1}{8}$ inches
3. $9\frac{1}{2}$
4. $8\frac{1}{2}$

4.

1. $56 - (\$24.93 + \$6.70 + \$6.70 + \$6) = \$11.67$
2. $18.21
3. 2
4. one t-shirt. He will have $10.71 left if he buys one t-shirt.

5.

1. $5.50
2. $16.69. No, she doesn't have enough money.
3. $41.70

4. $13.90. No, she can't afford it.
5. Yes, she can buy it because it costs $10.20. She will have $2.47 left.

6.

1. $16.99 x .095 = $1.61, $16.99 + $1.61 = $18.60
2. $18.60 + $4.99 = $23.59
3. $23.59 – $2.47 = $21.12
4. 5 weeks

Week	Original amount	Amount Left to Be Paid
1	$23.59	$18.59
2	$18.59	$13.59
3	$13.59	$8.59
4	$8.59	$3.59
5	$3.59	<$0

7.

1. 2 ¼ inches
2. 1 1/8 inch each time (2 ¼ = 9/4 , 9/4 / 2 = 9/8 = 1 ⅛)
3. ¾ inch/ 2 = ⅜ inch

8.

1. $46
2. $23
3. .20 x ((2 x $5.99) + $2.99 + $4.50 + $8.75) = $5.64

9.

1. d = 38.5 inches/3.14
   d = 12.26 inches
2. .5 inch + 18 inches + 12.26 inches + 18 inches + .5 inches = 49.26 inches

10.

1. 8 ¼ inches, to match the length of the middle piece.
2. 5 ¼ inches, to reach the same height as the rest of the pieces that make up the bag.

11.

1. No, it is not big enough.
2. No, she needs 13.26 more inches. (1 yard x 3 feet x 12 inches = 36 inches)
3. No
4. $(2 \times (5.25 \times 4.25)) + (2 \times (8.25 \times 5.25) + (8.25 \times 4.25) + (24 \times 2.5) = 226.31$ square inches
5. 810 square inches
6. Yes she has enough, yes she could get a ¼ yard, which is 405 square inches.

12.

1. $38.66
2. She will need to charge at least $26.24 to make a profit.
3. $135
4. $161.23. The dress seems expensive, and people might buy it.
5. $56.43. Yes, that seems fairer.

13.

1. She is making $7.32 more at the store
2. $17.50
3. 4 shirts

Item	Price	Store Commission	Rest
Dress	$75	$11.25	$63.75
Shirt	$50	$7.50	$42.50
Skirt	$50	$7.50	$42.50
Bag	$40	$6	$34

14.

1. $72.17, $43.87
2. $84.34
3. $24.60

15.

1. Junior's size 5.
2. 6 ½
3. $19.80 (.4 x $32.99 = $13.19, $32.99 – $13.19 = $19.80)
4. Yes, you can afford it and have more than $3 left. ($19.80 x $0.095 = $1.88, $19.80 + $1.88 = $21.68)
5. Yes, by 3 inches.
6. $6.50 x .2 = $1.30
7. No, you need just .3 inches more.
   inches of fabric length:
   .5 yard x 3 feet x 12 inches = 18 inches
   length needed:
   825 square inches = length x 45 inches
   length = 18.3 inches
8. $11.20

INDEX

ABOUT THE AUTHOR

Rae Simons is a well-established educational author, who has written on a variety of topics for young adults for the past twenty years.

Picture Credits